FEARLESS TRAILBLAZERS
PIONEROS AUDACES

11 Latinos who made U.S. History

11 Latinos que hicieron historia en Estados Unidos

Written by: NAIBE REYNOSO

Illustrated by: JONE LEAL

DEDICATION

To Brayden Mateo and all the fearless little boys and girls.

ISBN-13: 978-1733710350
Printed in the United States of America. First Printing, 2020.

CON TODO PRESS provides special discounts when purchased in larger volumes for premiums and promotional purposes, as well as for fundraising and educational use.
For more information, please contact contodopress@gmail.com

Publisher's Cataloging-in-Publication Data
Names: Reynoso, Naibe, author. | Leal, Jone, illustrator.
Title: Fearless trailblazers : 11 Latinos who made U.S. history / Pioneros audaces : 11 Latinos que hicieron historia en Estados Unidos / Naibe Reynoso ; illustrated by Jone Leal.
Description: Includes bibliographical references. | Los Angeles, CA: Con Todo Press, 2020.
Identifiers: LCCN: 2019921260 | ISBN: 978-1-7337103-5-0
Subjects: LCSH Hispanic Americans--Biography--Juvenile literature. | Hispanic Americans--History-- Juvenile literature. | United States--Civilization--Hispanic influences-- Juvenile literature. | CYAC Hispanic Americans--Biography. | Hispanic Americans--History. | United States--Civilization--Hispanic influences. | BISAC BIOGRAPHY & AUTOBIOGRAPHY / Cultural, Ethnic & Regional / Hispanic & Latino
Classification: LCC E184.S75 .R493 2020 | DDC 920/.009268--dc23

Translated by: Victoria Infante.
Graphic designer Alicia Freile.

CON TODO
PRESS

THIS BOOKS BELONGS TO:

_____

Cuando era niño, José Hernández soñaba al espacio volar.
Pero primero trabajó en el campo, mudándose de lugar en lugar.

Estudió ingeniería, matemáticas y ciencia porque tenía claro su destino.
Lo que le sirvió mucho para convertirse en astronauta y forjar su propio
      camino.

Con trabajo y persistencia, su sueño de la infancia se hizo realidad.
¡Viajó en un transbordador espacial gracias a su tenacidad!

JOSÉ HERNÁNDEZ
Astronaut

As a little boy, José Hernández dreamt of voyaging into space.
His journey began while harvesting crops and moving from place to place.

He earned top grades in his favorite subjects: engineering, science, and math.
Which served him greatly in becoming an astronaut and charting his
    own path!

With hard work and determination, his childhood dreams came true.
José traveled in a rocket ship, and with persistence, so can you!

Lin-Manuel Miranda es un compositor, dramaturgo y productor que
    resalta en los escenarios.
Hace musicales que nos educan y divierten, como "In the Heights"
    y "Hamilton", que son verdaderamente extraordinarios.

También es rapero, letrista, actor y cantante.
Tiene múltiples talentos. ¡Es una estrella brillante!

Ha ganado varios premios y la gente lo aclama.
Incluso tiene una estrella en el Paseo de la Fama.

LIN-MANUEL MIRANDA
Playwright

Composer, playwright, and producer, Lin-Manuel Miranda brightens the
  screen and stage.
His compelling musicals, *In the Heights* and *Hamilton*, entertain, enlighten,
  and engage!

He's also a rapper, a singer, a lyricist, and an actor!
Multi-talented and brilliant, he's got the "it" factor!

Lin-Manuel wins over hearts, achieves accolades, and earns critical acclaim.
Among them: Tony and Grammy awards and a star on the Hollywood
  Walk of Fame!

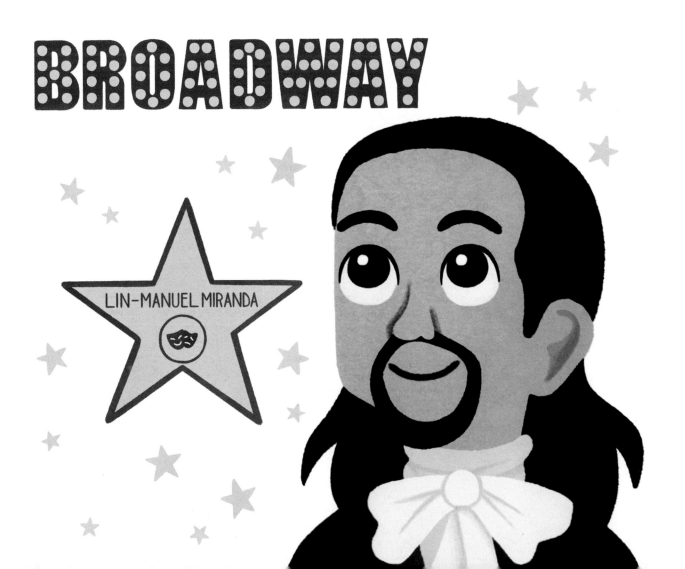

Albert Báez se mudó a Estados Unidos a los dos años, pero es mexicano
   de nacimiento.
Siempre amó las matemáticas y la física, ¡e hizo un gran descubrimiento!

Inventó un microscopio que los científicos todavía usan hoy en día.
Ayuda a examinar las células vivas con una potente radiografía.

Así que si te gusta la ciencia y deseas ser inventor...
Tú eres inteligente. ¡Piensa en grande y muestra tu esplendor!

ALBERT BÁEZ
Scientist and Inventor

Born in Mexico, Albert Báez immigrated to the U.S. when he was only two.
His lifelong passions were math and physics, which led to his discovering
   something new!

Years ago, he invented a microscope that scientists still use today!
His innovation helps examine living cells using a powerful X-ray.

If, like Albert, you love science, and it's a field that you want to enter,
Think big and use your smarts, as you may become our
   next inventor!

Fernando Valenzuela fue uno de los mejores lanzadores de su
   generación.
¡En sus diez años con los Dodgers, cautivó a toda la nación!

Su apodo era "El Toro" y tenía fans en todo el mundo.
Cada vez que subía al montículo, su éxito era rotundo.

Ganó el premio Cy Young y fue Novato del año. ¡Un hecho admirable!
Fue un campeón de la Serie Mundial y tuvo una carrera impecable.

FERNANDO VALENZUELA
Professional Baseball Player

Fernando Valenzuela is revered as one of the best pitchers of his
   generation!
During his decade playing for the Dodgers, he captivated the entire
   nation.

Nicknamed "El Toro," which in Spanish means The Bull,
Whenever he was pitching, the stadiums remained full!

Fernando won the Cy Young Award and was named Rookie of the Year!
A World Series champion, he had a remarkable career!

A los cinco años tocaba el violín y a los ocho la guitarra.
Su talento lo llevaría muy lejos. ¡Él es Carlos Santana!

Incluso hace cantar la guitarra, ¡su talento es divino!
Fusiona jazz, rock y ritmos afrocubanos con una mezcla de sonidos
    latinos.

También es humanista y ayuda a los necesitados.
Es una superestrella que da la mano a los menos afortunados.

CARLOS SANTANA
Musical Icon

At five, he played the violin, and at eight, he learned the guitar.
Carlos Santana's musical abilities have taken him very far.

He can make his guitar sing, his talents have no bounds.
Infusing jazz, rock, and Afro-Cuban rhythms with a mix of Latin sounds!

He's also a humanitarian, dedicated to helping those in need!
Santana's talent and generosity make him a superstar, indeed!

César Chávez fue un líder sindical que hizo de los derechos civiles
    su vocación.
Un campeón de los trabajadores agrícolas que entendió su difícil situación.

En defensa de los demás, su compasión alcanzó nuevas alturas.
Hasta el día de hoy, su mensaje resuena, empodera y une. ¡Sigue siendo
    una gran figura!

Es un verdadero héroe estadounidense que será recordado generación tras
    generación.
Su legado es importante y forma parte de la historia de nuestra nación.

CÉSAR CHÁVEZ
Civil Rights Activist

As a labor leader, César Chávez fought for civil rights.
A champion for farmworkers, he understood their plights.

Standing up for others, his compassion reached great heights.
And to this day, his message resonates, empowers, and unites!

A true American hero, Chávez will be remembered for generations.
His legacy is interwoven in the history of our nation.

Para Oscar de la Renta, desde niño el arte fue su pasión.
Pero a medida que creció, se dio cuenta de que la moda tenía su corazón.

Dignatarios y primeras damas portan sus diseños.
En los desfiles de moda, modelos y celebridades visten sus estilos
    de ensueño.

Conocido como el "Caballero de moda", era refinado y brillante.
Sus vestidos eran sencillos y a la vez elegantes.

OSCAR DE LA RENTA
Fashion Designer

As a young boy, Oscar de la Renta had an affinity for all forms of art.
While growing up, fashion became his calling, as it took hold of his heart!

Dignitaries and first ladies dress in his exquisite designer clothes.
Models and celebrities wear them in prestigious fashion shows!

Known as "the Gentleman of Fashion," he strove for elegance in his
  designs.
De la Renta had a gift for creating clothes that are timeless, classic, and
  refined.

Jean-Michel Basquiat fue un artista con herencia de Haití y Puerto Rico.
Sus pinturas están en los mejores museos. Su estilo era magnífico.

Su madre, Matilde, lo inspiró a que continuara su carrera en el arte
    desde que era muy niño.
En casa dibujaba, escribía y coloreaba, algo que hacía con mucho
    empeño y cariño.

Su diversa herencia cultural fue una fuente de inspiración.
Su trabajo continúa cautivando a cada generación.

JEAN-MICHEL BASQUIAT
Artist

Jean-Michel Basquiat was an artist of Haitian and Puerto Rican descent.
World-class museums display his paintings, as they are magnificent!

His mom, Matilde, inspired him to pursue his art when he was a little boy.
He would draw, and write, and color, that's what really brought him joy.

Pop culture and themes like race and class were his sources of inspiration.
Basquiat's thought-provoking art continues to captivate every generation!

Rubén Salazar fue un periodista que luchó por hacer brillar a su
    comunidad.
Escribía sobre lo que es ser latino en cada oportunidad.

Impulsado por el activismo por los derechos civiles, se unió al
    Movimiento Chicano.
En su columna en el diario Los Angeles Times, abogó por mejorar las
    condiciones del ser humano.

Tú también puedes usar tu voz para hacer cosas positivas.
Y hasta un cambio social puedes provocar con lo que escribas.

RUBÉN SALAZAR
Pioneering Journalist and Civil Rights Activist

Distinguished journalist, Rubén Salazar, shined a light on his community,
Covering news stories about the Latino experience at every opportunity.

Driven by civil rights activism, he joined the Chicano movement.
His column at the Los Angeles Times crusaded for social improvement.

Be outspoken, like Rubén was, using your voice to make things right!
When passionate about your purpose, even a cause you can ignite!

Ricardo Montalbán nació en México, donde destacó en la actuación.
Luego vino a Estados Unidos y retomó su carrera, algo que hizo con
la misma pasión.

Pronto consiguió papeles importantes en teatro, cine y programas
de televisión.
De comedia a drama, llegó hasta donde estaban los grandes de la profesión.

Pero su mayor regalo fue ayudar a otros actores latinos a través de
su fundación.
Abrió muchas puertas en Hollywood para la nueva generación.

RICARDO MONTALBÁN
Award-Winning Actor

Ricardo Montalbán was born in Mexico, where he became a famous actor.
And then, he moved to the United States to start a brand new chapter.

He soon had leading roles in theatre, film, and TV shows.
From comedy to drama, he was up there with the pros!

Perhaps his greatest gift was helping Latino actors through his Foundation.
Montalbán opened many doors in Hollywood for the younger generations.

¿Qué quieres ser cuando seas grande? ¡No tengas límites! ¡Sé valiente!
Todo es posible, incluso puedes postularte para ser presidente.

Como Julián Castro, quien cree que todos merecen una oportunidad.
De soñar en grande, alcanzar sus metas, y ayudar a su comunidad.

Graduado de la Facultad de Derecho de Harvard, trabajó en la
    administración del presidente Barack Obama.
¡Su madre lo impulsó a soñar en grande para que creara su propio
    panorama!

JULIÁN CASTRO
Politician

Julián Castro was mayor of San Antonio, Texas, working hard to serve its
   residents.
And then he had the grandest of dreams and even ran for President!

A Harvard Law School graduate, Julián worked for President Barack Obama.
His mother inspired him to have no limits and create his own life's panorama!

So what do YOU want to be when you grow up? Think BIG! Don't be hesitant!
Anything is Possible! You can even Run for PRESIDENT!

YOU / TÚ

Now look into the mirror, what's reflecting back your way?
Perhaps Julián, Lin-Manuel, Carlos, Ricardo, or José?

The answer is YOU! Kind, compassionate, and SMART!
Loving, deserving, whole and complete, YOU have a real big HEART!

So go out and be FEARLESS! Show your TALENTS! Don't be shy!
The world deserves your gifts, there are a million reasons why!

Like all these FEARLESS TRAILBLAZERS, who are now known far
    and wide,
You have unlimited potential, so let your PASSION be your guide!

Ahora mírate al espejo. ¿Qué es lo que ves reflejado?
¿Quizá Julián, Lin-Manuel, Carlos, José o Ricardo?

¡Eres TÚ! Amable, sensible e INTELIGENTE.
 Adorable, digno, completo y con un CORAZÓN gigante.

Sé VALIENTE, muestra tu ingenio. ¡No seas cohibido!
El mundo merece tus TALENTOS, esos con los que has nacido.

Como todos estos PIONEROS AUDACES, que son conocidos por todas
    partes hoy en día.
Tú tienes un gran potencial, ¡así que deja que tu PASIÓN sea tu guía!

BIOGRAPHIES/
BIOGRAFÍAS

ALBERT BÁEZ, a physicist, was born on November 12, 1912, in Puebla, Mexico. In 1950, he earned his doctorate in Physics at Stanford University, where he and Dr. Paul Kirkpatrick invented the X-ray reflection microscope, which today is still used for examining living cells. Báez was the first director of the science education programs offered by UNESCO, where he dedicated himself to improving access to STEM academic curriculums in Latin America, Asia, Africa, and the Middle East. Báez is the father of folk singers, Joan Báez and Mimi Fariña.

JEAN-MICHEL BASQUIAT, an artist, was born on December 22, 1960, in Brooklyn, New York. His father, Gerard Basquiat, was born in Haiti, and his mother, Matilde Andrades, was born in Brooklyn of Puerto Rican descent. Basquiat was brilliant, and at a young age, he was fluent in English, French, and Spanish. By the 1980s, his paintings were exhibited in galleries and museums worldwide. In 2017, one of Basquiat's paintings, "Untitled," which he created in 1982, broke records when it was sold at auction for $110.5 million.

JULIÁN CASTRO, a political figure and public servant, was born (alongside his twin brother, Joaquín), on September 16, 1974, in San Antonio, Texas. He holds a Juris Doctor degree from Harvard Law School, where he graduated in 2000. Julián was Mayor of San Antonio from 2009 to 2014, and Secretary of Housing and Urban Development from 2014 to 2017, under President Barack Obama. In 2019, he announced his presidential bid in the 2020 presidential election. While Julián has ended his campaign, no doubt, he will continue to make an impact via his career in public service.

CÉSAR ESTRADA CHÁVEZ, a civil rights activist, was born on March 31, 1927, near Yuma, Arizona. As a fearless union leader and labor organizer, he dedicated his life to improving work and pay conditions for farmworkers. In 1962, Chávez, along with Dolores Huerta, co-founded the National Farmworkers Association, which later became the United Farm Workers. In 2014, President Barack Obama announced that March 31st, Chávez's birthday, would be recognized as a federal commemorative holiday.

OSCAR DE LA RENTA, a fashion designer, was born on July 22, 1932, in the Dominican Republic. He was considered one of the world's leading high fashion designers, who dressed first ladies, including Jackie Kennedy, Nancy Reagan, Laura Bush, and Hillary Clinton, as well as many celebrities. In 1973, the Coty Hall of Fame inducted him. In 1989, the Council of Fashion Designers of America bestowed upon him the Lifetime Achievement Award.

JOSÉ HERNÁNDEZ, an engineer and astronaut, was born on August, 1962, in rural California. At a young age, he harvested crops with his parents, who were migrant farmworkers, and only learned to speak English when he was 12 years old. After graduating from high school, José pursued bachelor's and master's degrees in science-related fields. In 2004, he joined the NASA space program, and in 2009, he traveled into space aboard the shuttle Discovery. In 2005, José formed the Reaching for the Stars Foundation to encourage youth interest in STEM.

LIN-MANUEL MIRANDA, a composer, lyricist, singer, playwright, producer, and actor of Puerto Rican descent, was born on January 16, 1980, in New York City. Miranda has received critical acclaim for creating and starring in the Broadway smash hit musicals, In the Heights and Hamilton. In 2016, he won the Pulitzer Prize in Drama. He has also received numerous Grammy, Emmy, and Tony awards and in 2017 was been nominated for an Oscar. In 2018, Lin-Manuel was a recipient of the Kennedy Center Honors and was given a star on the Hollywood Walk of Fame.

RICARDO MONTALBÁN, an actor, was born on November 25, 1920, in Mexico City. After becoming a successful actor in Mexico, he moved to the United States, where he conquered Hollywood, becoming one of the entertainment industry's first Mexican-born screen legends. Later in life, he starred as Mr. Roarke in the popular television series, Fantasy Island, which aired from 1978 to 1984. In 1970, Montalbán also founded the nonprofit, Nosotros Foundation, to improve the image and increase the representation and employment of Latinos in Hollywood.

RUBÉN SALAZAR, a journalist, and activist, was born on March 3, 1928, in Ciudad Juárez, Mexico, and was raised in El Paso, Texas. In 1954, he graduated with a degree in journalism from Texas Western College. From 1959 to 1970, Rubén was a news reporter and columnist for the Los Angeles Times. During his distinguished career, he became one of the most prominent figures within the Chicano movement. In 1970, Rubén transitioned from print to broadcast, when he became News Director for the Spanish-language television station, KMEX.

CARLOS SANTANA, a musical icon, was born on July 20, 1947, in Autlán de Navarro, Mexico. When he was little, his father, who had a Mariachi band called Los Cardinales, taught him to play the violin and the guitar. Today, he is revered as one of the world's best electric guitarists. He is known for infusing jazz, rock, and Afro-Cuban rhythms with Latin sounds in his music. Also, he is the winner of 10 Grammy awards. In 1998, the Rock and Roll Hall of Fame inducted Santana. Moreover, for over two decades, the Milagro Foundation which he and his family created, has been providing aid to vulnerable children.

FERNANDO VALENZUELA, a professional baseball player, was born on November 1, 1960, in Sonora, Mexico. He played in the major leagues for 17 seasons, 11 of which were with the Los Angeles Dodgers. A phenomenal pitcher, he became the first player to win the Cy Young Award and be named Rookie of the Year in the same season. In 1981, after leading the Los Angeles Dodgers in their World Series title, Valenzuela's popularity skyrocketed and inspired avid fandom known as "Fernandomania."

NAIBE REYNOSO
Author

Naibe Reynoso is a Mexican-American multi-Emmy award-winning journalist with over two decades of career experience. Her work has been seen in CNN Español, France 24, Reelz Channel, Univision, Telemundo/KWHY, and Fox News Latino to name a few. She is also a board member of the prestigious Peabody Awards. She graduated from UCLA with a degree in Sociology, and a double concentration in Psychology and Chicano Studies. She lives in her native, Los Angeles, California with her teenage daughter, young son and husband Jeff.

To learn more about the author, go to naibereynoso.com or follow her on Instagram @naibereynoso

JONE LEAL
Illustrator

Jone Leal, also known as "jonewho" is a Venezuelan illustrator who loves to work with children's book illustrations and women empowerment. She has over 5 years of experience in the area. When she's not drawing, you can find her sewing while listening to her favorite music. She also illustrated "Be Bold! Be Brave! 11 Latinas who made U.S. History." To see more of her work visit jonewho.com or follow her on Instagram @jonewho

To learn more about CON TODO PRESS
visit contodopress.com or follow @contodopress

BIBLIOGRAPHY/
BIBLIOGRAFÍA

http://astrojh.org/astronaut-jose-m-hernandez

https://www.thoughtco.com/former-nasa-astronaut-jose-hernandez-biography-2834889

https://www.nasa.gov/audience/forstudents/nasaandyou/home/jose_bkgd_en.html

https://www.linmanuel.com/

https://www.craftonhills.edu/features/hispanic-heritage-month-2014/hispanic-heritage-profiles/albert-baez.php

https://www.geni.com/people/Albert-Baez/6000000009920306233

https://archive.is/20121214205815/http://www.hmc.edu/newsandevents/albertbaezobit.html#selection-327.0-327.172

https://woub.org/2019/09/27/ruben-salazar-man-in-the-middle-voces-on-pbs-friday-october-4-at-10-pm/

https://www.democracynow.org/2010/8/31/slain_latino_journalist_ruben_salazar_killed

https://www.santana.com/carlos-santana-biography/

https://www.rollingstone.com/music/music-news/the-epic-life-of-carlos-santana-89485/

https://www.thesound.co.nz/home/music/2018/07/8-interesting-facts-about-rock-legend-carlos-santana.html

https://ufw.org/research/history/story-cesar-chavez/

https://www.biography.com/activist/cesar-chavez

https://www.nytimes.com/2014/10/21/nyregion/oscar-de-la-renta-fashion-designer-dies-at-82.html

https://www.nytimes.com/2014/10/23/fashion/oscar-de-la-renta-legacy.
          html?action=click&module=RelatedCoverage&pgtype=Article&region=Footer

https://www.julianforthefuture.com/

https://www.businessinsider.com/who-is-julian-castro-bio-age-family-key-positions-2019-3

https://www.latimes.com/local/obituaries/la-me-montalban15-2009jan15-story.html

https://www.mlb.com/player/fernando-valenzuela-123619

https://www.britannica.com/biography/Fernando-Valenzuela

https://www.latimes.com/sports/dodgers/story/2019-07-20/dodgers-fernando-valenzuela

https://www.latimes.com/local/obituaries/la-me-montalban15-2009jan15-story.html

https://www.biography.com/news/jean-michael-basquiat-black-artists

https://www.biography.com/political-figure/julian-castro

http://www.basquiat.com/

http://movies2.nytimes.com/books/98/08/09/specials/basquiat-mag.html